9/13

PIONEERS IN ASTRONOMY AND SPACE EXPLORATION

PIONEERS IN ASTRONOMY AND SPACE EXPLORATION

EDITED BY MICHAEL ANDERSON

Britannica
Educational Publishing
IN ASSOCIATION WITH

ROSEN
EDUCATIONAL SERVICES

Published in 2013 by Britannica Educational Publishing
(a trademark of Encyclopædia Britannica, Inc.)
in association with Rosen Educational Services, LLC
29 East 21st Street, New York, NY 10010.

Distributed exclusively by Rosen Educational Services.
For a listing of additional Britannica Educational Publishing titles, call toll free (800) 237-9932.

First Edition

Britannica Educational Publishing
J.E. Luebering: Director, Core Reference Group, Encyclopædia Britannica
Adam Augustyn: Assistant Manager, Encyclopædia Britannica

Anthony L. Green: Editor, Compton's by Britannica
Michael Anderson: Senior Editor, Compton's by Britannica
Andrea R. Field: Senior Editor, Compton's by Britannica
Sherman Hollar: Senior Editor, Compton's by Britannica

Marilyn L. Barton: Senior Coordinator, Production Control
Steven Bosco: Director, Editorial Technologies
Lisa S. Braucher: Senior Producer and Data Editor
Yvette Charboneau: Senior Copy Editor
Kathy Nakamura: Manager, Media Acquisition

Rosen Educational Services
Jeanne Nagle: Senior Editor
Nelson Sá: Art Director
Cindy Reiman: Photography Manager
Karen Huang: Photo Researcher
Brian Garvey: Designer, Cover Design
Introduction by Jeanne Nagle

Library of Congress Cataloging-in-Publication Data

Pioneers in astronomy and space exploration/edited by Michael Anderson.—1st ed.
    p. cm.—(Inventors and innovators)
"In association with Britannica Educational Publishing, Rosen Educational Services."
Audience: Grade 7 to 8
Includes bibliographical references and index.
ISBN 978-1-61530-695-4 (lib. bdg.)
1. Astronomers—Biography—Juvenile literature. 2. Astrophysicists—Biography—
Juvenile literature. 3. Astronomy—History—Juvenile literature. 4. Astronautics—History—
Juvenile literature. I. Anderson, Michael, 1972–
QB35.P56 2013
520.92'2—dc23

2012003790

Manufactured in the United States of America

On the cover, page 3: *Apollo 11 astronaut Buzz Aldrin standing on the surface of the Moon, 1969.* NASA/
Photo Researchers/Getty Images

Interior background image © iStockphoto.com/alxpin

CONTENTS

INTRODUCTION

Astronaut Edwin ("Buzz") Aldrin, Jr., pilot of the Gemini 12 spacecraft, performing an extravehicular activity (EVA) on Nov. 12, 1966, the second day of the four-day mission in space. Aldrin is positioned next to the Agena workstation. NASA Great Images in Nasa Collection

Pioneers are bold and daring individuals who go where no one has been, or only few others have gone, before. Pioneering can be mental, where someone explores the unknown using theory, as well as physical, where a person actually travels to distant locations. The pioneers of astronomy and space exploration fall into both camps. As this book details, astronomers through the centuries have attempted to explain mysteries of the universe using observation and scientific theory, with their feet planted firmly on Earth. Beginning in the 20th century, however, men and women boarded rocket ships and were launched into space for firsthand exploration.

Ancient astronomers weren't the first people to notice, or even wonder about, the Sun, Moon, and stars. They were, however, the first to apply scientific reason and order to the universe. Considered the earliest astronomer, Eudoxus of Cnidus recorded the positions and dates of visibility for constellations. He also concluded that the Sun, Moon, and known planets traveled in consistent paths, or orbits—although he was off the mark when he claimed that Earth was the center of all this activity.

Many of the great thinkers of the time, including Aristotle, based their work on Eudoxus's model of the universe, amending various parts as new information came to light. This set the pattern for the advancement of astronomy as a science, with new theories building on those that came before. Hipparchus and Ptolemy used the methods devised by Aristarchus of Samos in an attempt to figure out the size of the Moon and its distance from Earth. Also influenced by Aristarchus was the father of modern astronomy, Nicolaus Copernicus, whose own theories were later championed by Galileo. Tycho Brahe shared his data with Johannes Kepler, who, in turn, greatly influenced Sir Isaac Newton.

Intrigued by the observations of astronomers (and, in some cases, by science fiction stories as well), physicists and engineers of the 20th century developed the technology that would allow for exploration in space. The work of Robert H. Goddard, Wernher von Braun, and other rocket scientists led to spacecraft that would launch humans into orbit.

The earliest pioneers who rode those rockets into space came from the former

Soviet Union (now Russia) and the United States. In a race to space, each country tried to outdo the other with its achievements in exploring the so-called final frontier. Soviet cosmonaut Yury Gagarin won the title of first human in space over American astronauts Alan B. Shepherd, who made a suborbital flight about three weeks after Gagarin's flight, and John Glenn, the first American to orbit Earth. Americans, however, were first to land on the Moon, where Neil Armstrong and Buzz Aldrin explored the surface and planted an American flag.

Women also made their mark as space explorers. Valentina Tereshkova of the Soviet Union was the first woman to travel in space, while Sally Ride was the first American woman to do so. Although tragedy cut her journey short of its goal, teacher Christa McAullife was chosen as the first private citizen to travel into space, aboard the U.S. space shuttle *Challenger*.

These days space pioneering is done mostly by unmanned satellites, which travel to distant locations and beam images back to Earth. Yet humans may once again venture deep into space, spurred on by the accomplishments of pioneers from days gone by.

CHAPTER 1

EUDOXUS OF CNIDUS

A Greek mathematician and astronomer, Eudoxus of Cnidus contributed to the identification of constellations, and thus to the development of astronomy in ancient Greece. He also established the first sophisticated model of planetary motion.

Eudoxus was born around 395–390 BCE in Cnidus, Asia Minor (now in Turkey). He studied mathematics and medicine, and later went to Athens, where he took part in philosophical discussions at the famous Academy directed by the philosopher Plato. He eventually returned to Cnidus, where he became a legislator and continued his research until his death at age 53.

In his astronomical works, Eudoxus mapped out the constellations and described the phases of fixed stars (the dates when they are visible). He also discussed the sizes of the Sun, Moon, and Earth. Perhaps Eudoxus's greatest fame stems from his being the first to create a geometric model of the motions of the Sun, the Moon, and the five planets known in ancient times. His model consisted of a complex system of 27 interconnected spheres with Earth at the center. One sphere held the fixed stars, while each planet occupied four spheres and the Sun and Moon had three each. Callippus and later Aristotle modified the model. Aristotle's endorsement of its basic principles guaranteed an enduring interest through the Renaissance.

Most astronomers seem to have abandoned the astronomical views of Eudoxus by the middle of the 2nd century BCE. Nevertheless, his principle that every celestial motion is uniform and circular around the center endured until the time of the 17th-century astronomer Johannes Kepler.

CHAPTER 2

ARISTOTLE

The ancient Greek philosopher Aristotle ranks among the greatest thinkers of all time. His work in the natural and social sciences greatly influenced virtually every area of modern thinking.

LIFE

Aristotle was born in 384 BCE in Stagira, on the northwest coast of the Aegean Sea. His father was a friend and the physician of the king of Macedonia, and the boy spent most of his childhood at the court. At age 17 he went to Athens to study, where he enrolled at Plato's Academy. Plato was soon calling him the "mind of the school." Aristotle stayed at the Academy for 20 years, leaving only when his beloved master died in 347 BCE. In later years he renounced some of Plato's theories and went far beyond him in breadth of knowledge.

Aristotle became a teacher in a school on the coast of Asia Minor. He spent two years studying marine biology on Lesbos. In 342 BCE Philip II invited Aristotle to return to the Macedonian court and teach his 13-year-old son, Alexander, who was to become the world conqueror Alexander the Great. After Alexander became king, he gave Aristotle a large sum of money to set up a school in Athens.

Aristotle with a Bust of Homer, *a painting by Rembrandt. Aristotle's view of the cosmos incorporated elements of earlier scientific and philosophical theories concerning the universe.* Photos.com/Thinkstock

In Athens Aristotle taught brilliantly at his school in a sacred grove called the Lyceum. He collected the first great library and established a museum. In the mornings he strolled in the Lyceum gardens, discussing problems with his advanced students. He led his pupils in research in every existing field of knowledge. In fact, one of Aristotle's most important contributions was defining and classifying the various branches of knowledge: physics, metaphysics, psychology, rhetoric, poetics, and logic. Thus he laid the foundation of most of the sciences of today.

Anti-Macedonian feeling broke out in Athens in 323 BCE. The Athenians accused Aristotle of impiety, or lacking proper respect. He chose to flee so that the Athenians might not "twice sin against philosophy" by killing him as they had fellow ancient philosopher Socrates. He fled to Chalcis on the island of Euboea. There he died the next year.

CONCEPTION OF THE UNIVERSE

In a number of works Aristotle presented a world-picture that included many features inherited from his predecessors. From the philosopher Empedocles he adopted the view that the universe is composed of different combinations of the four fundamental elements of earth, water, air, and fire. Each element possesses a unique pair of the four elementary qualities of heat, cold, wetness, and dryness: earth is cold and dry, water is cold and wet, air is hot and wet, and fire is hot and dry. Each element has a natural place in an ordered cosmos, and each has a tendency to move toward this natural place. Thus, earthy solids naturally fall, while fire, unless prevented, rises ever higher.

Aristotle's vision of the cosmos also owes much to Plato's dialogue *Timaeus*. As in that work, Earth is at the center of the universe, and the Moon, the Sun, and the other planets revolve around it in concentric spheres. The heavenly bodies are not compounds of the four basic elements but are made up of a superior fifth element, or "quintessence." In addition, the heavenly bodies have souls, or supernatural intellects, which guide them in their travels through the cosmos.

Scientists now know that Aristotle's ideas about astronomy are inaccurate.

Nevertheless, he is considered the first genuine scientist in history, and his influence was immense. He was the first author whose surviving works contain detailed observations of natural phenomena. He also was the first philosopher to have a sound grasp of the relationship between observation and theory in scientific method.

CHAPTER 3

ARISTARCHUS OF SAMOS

A Greek astronomer of the 3rd cen-tury BCE, Aristarchus of Samos was the pioneer of the theory that the Sun is at the center of the universe and that Earth revolves around it. This heliocentric, or Sun-centered, model of the solar system never gained wide support in the ancient world. It was not until the 16th century that the idea began to be reestablished.

Aristarchus's only surviving work is *On the Sizes and Distances of the Sun and Moon.* Starting with the size of Earth's shadow cast on the Moon during a lunar eclipse, Aristarchus calculated the size of the Moon relative to Earth. From its measured angular size, he then obtained the distance to the Moon. He also proposed a clever scheme to measure the size of and distance to the Sun. Although flawed, the method did enable him to deduce that the Sun is much larger than Earth. This deduction led Aristarchus to speculate that Earth revolves about the Sun rather than the other way around.

Later Greek astronomers, especially Hipparchus and Ptolemy, refined Aristarchus's methods and arrived at very accurate values for the size of and distance to the Moon. However, all ancient results greatly underestimated the size of and distance to the Sun.

In the 16th century Aristarchus was an inspiration for the work of Polish astronomer Nicolaus Copernicus. In his manuscript of *On the Revolutions of the Celestial Spheres* (1543), Copernicus cited Aristarchus as an ancient authority who had put forth the idea that Earth is in motion. However, Copernicus later crossed out this reference, and Aristarchus's theory was not mentioned in the published book.

CHAPTER 4

HIPPARCHUS

Aprolific and talented Greek astronomer, Hipparchus made fundamental
contributions to the advancement of astronomy as a mathematical science. He also
helped to lay the foundations of trigonometry. Although he is commonly ranked
among the greatest scientists of antiquity,
very little is known about his life, and only
one of his many writings is still in existence.
Knowledge of the rest of his work relies on
second-hand reports, especially in the great
astronomical manual called the *Almagest*,
written by Ptolemy in the 2nd century CE.

Born in Nicaea, Bithynia (now Iznik,
Turkey), Hipparchus lived in the 2nd century BCE. As a young man he compiled
records of local weather patterns throughout the year. Most of his adult life, however,
seems to have been spent carrying out
astronomical observations and research on
the Greek island of Rhodes.

Hipparchus's most important astronomical work concerned the orbits of

the Sun and Moon, a determination of their sizes and distances from Earth, and the study of eclipses. Like most of his predecessors—Aristarchus of Samos was an exception—Hipparchus assumed that Earth was stationary at the center of the universe and that the Sun, Moon, planets, and stars revolved around it each day.

Every year the Sun traces out a circular path in a west-to-east direction relative to the stars. Hipparchus had good reasons for believing that the Sun's path, known as the ecliptic, is a great circle—that is, that the plane of the ecliptic passes through Earth's center. The two points at which the ecliptic and the equatorial plane intersect are known as the vernal and autumnal equinoxes. The two points of the ecliptic farthest north and south from the equatorial plane are known as the summer and winter solstices. The equinoxes and solstices divide the ecliptic into four equal parts, or seasons. However, the Sun's passage through each section of the ecliptic is not symmetrical. Hipparchus discovered a method of using the dates of two equinoxes and a solstice to calculate the size and direction of the displacement of the

The Greek astronomer Hipparchus, gazing skyward. Among Hipparchus's astronomical accomplishments were measuring the distances of the Sun and the Moon from Earth, and creating the first star catalog. Archive Photos/Getty Images

Sun's orbit. With Hipparchus's mathematical model, one could calculate not only the Sun's orbital location on any date, but also its position as seen from Earth.

Hipparchus also tried to measure as precisely as possible the length of the tropical year—the period for the Sun to complete one passage through the ecliptic. He made observations of consecutive equinoxes and solstices and compared them with observations made in the 5th and 3rd centuries BCE. This led him to an estimate of the tropical year that was only 6 minutes too long.

Hipparchus was then able to calculate equinox and solstice dates for any year. Applying this information to observations from about 150 years before his time, he made the discovery that the positions of certain stars had shifted from the earlier measures. This indicated that Earth, not the stars, was moving. This movement, called precession, is a slow wobble in the orientation of Earth's axis caused by the gravity of the Sun and the Moon. The phenomenon discovered by Hipparchus is now known as the precession of the equinoxes.

In his studies of the motion of the Moon, Hipparchus estimated the Moon's size and distance from Earth. He noted that when a solar eclipse had been seen to be total in the Hellespont region of what is now western Turkey, only four-fifths of the Sun's disk had been covered as seen from Alexandria, Egypt. Using early trigonometry and knowing the approximate distance between these two places, he was able to calculate the Moon's distance as roughly 63 times Earth's radius. (The actual value is about 60 times.)

Hipparchus also created the first known star catalog, which assigned names to each star, and gave his measurements of each star's position. The catalog listed about 850 stars and specified their brightnesses by a system of six magnitudes that is similar to today's method of classification.

CHAPTER 5

PTOLEMY

Claudius Ptolemaeus, known as Ptolemy, was an eminent astronomer, mathematician, and geographer who lived in the 2nd century CE. He was of Greek descent but worked mostly in Alexandria, Egypt. In several fields his writings represent the greatest achievement of Greco-Roman science, particularly his Earth-centered model of the universe now known as the Ptolemaic system.

Virtually nothing is known about Ptolemy's life except what can be inferred from his writings. He was born in about 100 CE. His first major astronomical work, the *Almagest*, was completed around 150 CE and contains astronomical observations that Ptolemy had made over the preceding quarter of a century. The size and content of his subsequent literary production suggests that he lived until about 170 CE.

In the *Almagest*, Ptolemy lays out his argument that Earth is a stationary sphere at

The ancient astronomer Ptolemy, who developed what is now known as the Ptolemaic system of the universe—wherein the Sun, Moon, and planets revolve around a stationary Earth. © Image Asset Management Ltd./SuperStock

the center of a vastly larger celestial sphere that revolves at a perfectly uniform rate around Earth. The celestial sphere carries with it the stars, planets, Sun, and Moon, thereby causing their daily risings and settings. Through the course of a year the Sun slowly traces out a great orbit, the ecliptic, against the rotation of the celestial sphere. The basic assumption of the *Almagest* is that the apparently irregular movements of the heavenly bodies are actually combinations of regular, uniform, circular motions.

How much of the *Almagest* is original is difficult to determine. Ptolemy credited Hipparchus with essential elements of his solar theory, as well as parts of his lunar theory, while denying that Hipparchus constructed planetary models.

Ptolemy was preeminently responsible for the Earth-centered cosmology that prevailed in the Islamic world and in medieval Europe. This was not due to the *Almagest* so much as a later treatise, *Planetary Hypotheses*. In this work he proposed what is now called the Ptolemaic system. This is a unified system in which each heavenly body is attached to its own sphere, and the set of spheres is nested so

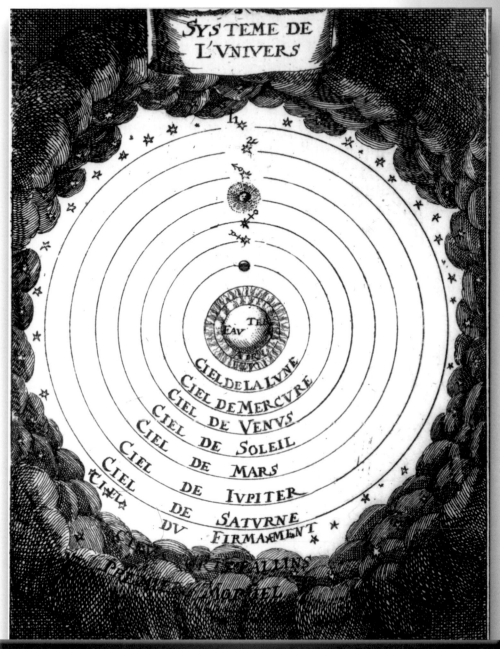

SYSTEME DE L'VNIVERS

CIEL DE LA LVNE
CIEL DE MERCVRE
CIEL DE VENVS
CIEL DE SOLEIL
CIEL DE MARS
CIEL DE IVPITER
CIEL DV SATVRNE
FIRMAMENT

Chart of the Ptolemaic system. Hulton Archive/Getty Images

that it extends without gaps from Earth to the celestial sphere. The Ptolemaic system was the official dogma of Western Christendom until the 1500s, when it was replaced by Nicolaus Copernicus's Sun-centered system.

Ptolemy has a prominent place in the history of mathematics primarily because of the mathematical methods he applied to astronomical problems. His contributions to trigonometry are especially important.

Ptolemy's fame as a geographer is hardly less than his fame as an astronomer. His eight-volume work *Guide to Geography* provides information on mapmaking and lists places in Europe, Asia, and Africa by latitude and longitude. In spite of its many errors, this work greatly influenced succeeding generations of geographers and mapmakers.

CHAPTER 6

NICOLAUS COPERNICUS

The Polish astronomer Nicolaus Copernicus is considered by many to be the founder of modern astronomy. His study led to his theory that Earth and the other planets revolve around the Sun. This representation of the heavens is usually called the heliocentric, or Sun-centered, system. Copernicus's theory had important consequences for later thinkers of the scientific revolution, including such major figures as Galileo, Johannes Kepler, and Isaac Newton.

Copernicus was born on Feb. 19, 1473, in Torun, Poland. His father was a well-to-do merchant, and his mother also came from a leading merchant family. After his father's death, the boy was raised by his uncle, a wealthy Catholic bishop, who sent him to the University of Kraków. There he studied liberal arts, including astronomy and astrology. Copernicus also studied law at Bologna and medicine at Padua in Italy.

Following his studies, he became an officer in the Roman Catholic church. In 1500

Nicolaus Copernicus, the founder of modern astronomy. Bucking commonly held beliefs, Copernicus determined that the Sun, not Earth, was the center of the universe.
Photos.com/Thinkstock

he lectured on mathematical subjects in Rome. He returned to his uncle's castle near Frauenburg in 1507 as attending physician to the elder man. Copernicus's astronomical work took place in his spare time, apart from his other obligations.

For centuries before Copernicus's time, astronomy had been based on the Ptolemaic theory that Earth was the center of the universe and motionless. Explaining how the other planets and heavenly bodies moved was problematic. At first it was thought that they simply moved in circular orbits around Earth. Calculations based on this view, however, did not agree with actual observations. Then it was thought that the other planets traveled in small circular orbits. These, in turn, were believed to move along larger orbits around Earth. However, within this theory, it could not be proved that Earth was the center of the universe.

Copernicus's revolutionary idea was that Earth should be regarded as one of the planets that revolved around the Sun. He also stated that Earth rotated on an axis. He did, however, still cling to the idea that planets traveled in small circular orbits that moved along larger orbits.

Copernicus probably hit upon his main idea sometime between 1508 and 1514. However, the historic book that contains the final version of his theory, *On the Revolutions of the Celestial Spheres*, did not appear in print until 1543, the year of his death.

CHAPTER 7

TYCHO BRAHE

The Danish astronomer Tycho Brahe was a pioneer in developing astronomical instruments, as well as measuring and fixing the positions of stars. His observations—the most accurate possible before the invention of the telescope—included a comprehensive study of the solar system and accurate positions of more than 777 fixed stars.

Brahe was born in the Scania region of Denmark on Dec. 14, 1546. His education began with the study of law at the University of Copenhagen from 1559 through 1562. Several important natural events turned him from law to astronomy. The first was the total eclipse of the Sun predicted for Aug. 21, 1560. Such a prediction seemed bold and marvelous to a 14-year-old student. Yet when Brahe witnessed the actual eclipse, he became an astronomy convert. His subsequent student life was divided between his daytime lectures on law, in response to the wishes of his uncle, and his nighttime vigil of the stars. His mathematics professor helped him with the only printed astronomical book available, Ptolemy's *Almagest*.

In 1562 Brahe's uncle sent him to the University of Leipzig, where he studied until 1565. Another significant event in the young man's life occurred in August 1563, when he made his first recorded observation, a conjunction, or alignment, of Jupiter and Saturn. Almost immediately he found that the existing almanacs and ephemerides, which record the positions of stars and planets, were grossly inaccurate. The Copernican tables were several days off in predicting this event. In his youthful enthusiasm Brahe decided to devote his life to accumulating accurate observations of the heavens in order to correct the existing tables.

Somewhere between 1565 and 1570 Brahe traveled widely throughout Europe, studying and acquiring mathematical and astronomical instruments. After inheriting the estates of his father and an uncle, he settled in Scania in about 1571 and built a small observatory. Here occurred the third and most important astronomical event in Brahe's life. On Nov. 11, 1572, he suddenly

Tycho Brahe (seated), shown consulting with fellow astronomer Johannes Kepler.
Transcendental Graphics/Archive Photos/Getty Images

saw a "new star," brighter than Venus and located where no star was supposed to be, in the constellation Cassiopeia. He carefully observed the new star and showed that it lay beyond the Moon, and therefore was in the realm of the fixed stars.

At the time this was an alarming discovery because since ancient times the stars had been regarded as perfect and unchanging. The news that a star could change as dramatically as that described by Brahe, together with reports of the Copernican theory that the Sun, not Earth, was the center of the universe, shook confidence in ancient knowledge. Brahe's discovery of the new star in 1572 and the publication of his observations in 1573 made him a respected astronomer throughout Europe.

The new star in the constellation Cassiopeia caused Brahe to rededicate himself to astronomy. King Frederick II of Denmark granted him financial support to build a large observatory, as well as an island on which to build it. Surrounded by scholars and visited by learned travelers from all over Europe, Brahe and his assistants collected observations and corrected nearly every known astronomical record.

After King Frederick died in 1588, Brahe's influence dwindled and most of his financial support was stopped. He left the observatory in 1597 and eventually settled in Prague. There he tried to continue his observations with the few instruments he had salvaged from the observatory. The spirit was not there, however, and he died on Oct. 24, 1601. He left all his observational data to Johannes Kepler, his pupil and assistant in the final years. With these data Kepler would lay the groundwork for the work of Isaac Newton.

CHAPTER 8

GALILEO

M odern physics owes its beginning to Galileo, who was the first astronomer to use a telescope. By discovering four satellites of the planet Jupiter, he gave visual evidence that supported the Copernican theory. Galileo thus helped disprove much of the medieval thinking in science.

Galileo Galilei, who is generally known only by his first name, was born in Pisa, Italy, on Feb. 15, 1564. His family belonged to the nobility but was not rich. His father sent him to study medicine at the local university. Galileo, however, soon turned to a career in science.

In 1583 Galileo discovered the law of the pendulum by watching a chandelier swing in the cathedral at Pisa. He timed it with his pulse and found that, whether it swung in a wide or a narrow arc, it always took the same time to complete an oscillation. He thus gave society the first reliable means of keeping time.

A lecture on geometry kindled his interest in mathematics, and he got his father's consent to change his studies. Lack of money forced him to leave school in 1585, and he became a lecturer at the Academy of Florence. The next year he attracted attention with discoveries in hydrostatics, which is a branch of physics that deals with the characteristics of fluids. His work in dynamics won him an appointment as lecturer on mathematics at the University of Pisa in 1589.

He soon made enemies with his arguments against what he considered mistakes in the science of the day. According to a popular story, he dropped weights from the leaning tower of Pisa to prove his views concerning falling bodies. His writings, however, do not mention such an experiment. In any case, resentment against his views drove him out of Pisa in 1591.

In 1592 the University of Padua offered Galileo a professorship in mathematics. About 1609, after word from Holland of Hans Lippershey's newly invented telescope reached him, he built his own version of the instrument. Galileo developed magnifying power until, on Jan. 7, 1610, he saw four satellites of Jupiter. He also saw the mountains and craters on the Moon and found the Milky Way to be a dense collection of stars.

Galileo moved to Florence in September 1610, working as a philosopher and mathematician. The year before, Johannes Kepler had published his laws of planetary motion based upon the Copernican theory. Galileo supported this view strongly. In 1616 he received a formal warning that the theory was contrary to the teachings of the church. Nevertheless, he again supported the Copernican view in a dialogue, *The Great Systems of the Universe*.

During his last eight years Galileo lived near Florence under house arrest for having "held and taught" Copernican doctrine. He became blind in 1637 but continued to work until his death on Jan. 8, 1642. Nearly 342 years later, Galileo was pardoned by Pope John Paul II, and the Roman Catholic church finally accepted his teachings.

Galileo's contributions to mechanics include the law of falling bodies, the fact that the path of a projectile is a parabola, the demonstration of the laws of equilibrium, and the principle of flotation. He devised a

Galileo, the first person credited with using a telescope for astronomical observation. Based on his observations and experiments, Galileo was able to disprove many scientific theories of his day. Science Source/Photo Researchers/Getty Images

simple thermometer and inspired a pupil, Evangelista Torricelli, to invent the barometer. His great contribution to scientific thinking was the principle of inertia. Before his time everyone followed Aristotle's theory that when an object moved, something had to act continuously to keep it moving. Galileo countered this with the theory that if a body is moving freely, something must happen to stop it or to make it change direction.

CHAPTER 9

JOHANNES KEPLER

The Renaissance astronomer and astrologer Johannes Kepler is best known for his discovery that the orbits in which Earth and the other planets of the solar system travel around the Sun are elliptical, or oval, in shape. He was also the first to explain correctly how human beings see and to demonstrate what happens to light when it enters a telescope. In addition, he designed an instrument that serves as the basis of the modern refractive telescope.

Kepler was born on Dec. 27, 1571, at Weil der Stadt in the duchy of Württemberg, now in southern Germany. He was a sickly child but had a brilliant mind. At the University of Tübingen he was greatly influenced by the theories of the astronomer Nicolaus Copernicus. He later taught astronomy and mathematics at the university in Graz, Austria. While there he corresponded with two other great astronomers of the time — Galileo and Tycho Brahe. In 1600 he became Brahe's assistant in Prague.

Greatly influenced by the work of Copernicus, Johannes Kepler is noted mainly for his discovery of the elliptical nature of planetary orbits within the solar system. SSPL via Getty Images

When Brahe died, Kepler succeeded him as astrologer and astronomer to Rudolph II of Bohemia. His task of doing horoscopes at births and other important events in the royal family was of first importance; astronomy was secondary.

Yet Kepler gave all the time he could to the outstanding astronomical problem of the day. By Kepler's time, many astronomers had accepted that the Sun was the center of the solar system and that Earth turned on its axis, but they still believed that the planets moved in circular orbits. Because of this, they could not explain the motions of the planets as seen from Earth. Kepler decided to try explaining these motions by finding another shape for the planetary orbits.

Kepler began with Mars because the planet offered the most typical problem, plus he had Brahe's accurate observations of Mars. Kepler tried every possible combination of circular motions in an attempt to account for Mars's positions. These all failed, though he once experienced a discrepancy of only eight unaccounted minutes of arc.

After six years, hampered by poor eyesight and the clumsy mathematical methods of the day, he found the answer. Mars follows an elliptical orbit at a speed that varies according to the planet's distance from the Sun. In 1609 Kepler published a book on the results of his work, boldly titling it *The New Astronomy*.

He then turned to the other planets and found that their motions corresponded to those of Mars. He also discovered that their periods of revolution—the time required to go around the Sun—bore a precise relation to their distances from the Sun.

Kepler's great work on planetary motion is summed up in three principles, which have become known as "Kepler's laws." The first law is that the path of every planet in its motion around the Sun forms an ellipse, with the Sun at one focus. The second law states that the speed of a planet in its orbit varies so that a line joining it with the Sun sweeps over equal areas in equal times. Finally, the third law concerns the squares of the planets' periods of revolution, which are proportional to the cubes of the planets' mean distances from the Sun. These laws removed all doubt that Earth and the planets of the solar system go around the Sun. Later Isaac Newton used Kepler's laws to establish his law of universal gravitation.

Having established these principles, Kepler could then proceed with his task of revising the *Tabulae Rudolphinae* (*Rudolphine Tables*), an almanac of the positions of heavenly bodies that, though unsatisfactory, was the best available at the time. Kepler's new laws enabled him to predict the positions of the planets by date and hour. These have proved to be substantially accurate even to the present day.

Kepler was one of the first to be informed by Galileo about his invention of the telescope; subsequently, the former went on to do valuable pioneer work in optics. It was Kepler who invented the present-day form of astronomical telescope. His book on optics, *Dioptrics*, published in 1611, was the first of its kind, founding the scientific study of light and lenses. Kepler died on Nov. 15, 1630, in Regensburg in Bavaria.

CHAPTER 10

GIAN DOMENICO CASSINI

The Italian-born astronomer Gian Domenico Cassini was the first in a four-generation dynasty of scientists who served as director of the Paris Observatory. He is known for his observations of the planets and their moons.

Gian Domenico Cassini was born in Perinaldo, Genoa, on June 8, 1625. He was educated by Jesuits and in 1650 became professor of astronomy at the University of Bologna. For many years he studied comets and other phenomena, but in 1664 he obtained a telescope that allowed him to make more detailed observations. In that year Cassini was able to measure Jupiter's rotational period, or the amount of time it takes the planet to rotate once about its axis, by studying the shadows of Jupiter's moons as they passed between that planet and the Sun.

In 1666, after a similar study of Mars, Cassini measured that planet's rotational period accurate to within three minutes of the time now known. Two years later he compiled a table of the positions of Jupiter's moons that was used in 1675 by another astronomer to establish that the speed of light is finite.

In 1671 Cassini was named director of the newly completed Paris Observatory. He became a French citizen in 1673 and changed his name to Jean-Dominique Cassini. Between 1671 and 1684 he discovered four of Saturn's moons. In 1675 he discovered the dark gap between rings A and B of Saturn. This gap was later named the Cassini Division. His theory that Saturn's rings were swarms of tiny moonlets too small to be seen individually has since been confirmed.

Cassini died in Paris on Sept. 14, 1712. In 2004 a spacecraft named in his honor became the first space probe to orbit Saturn.

Cassini's son, Jacques Cassini, compiled the first tables of the orbital motions of Saturn's moons in 1716. Jacques's son, César-François Cassini de Thury, continued the work begun by his father and also began a great topographical map of France. His son, Jacques-Dominique, comte de Cassini, completed the map of France begun by his father.

CHAPTER 11

CHRISTIAAN HUYGENS

The shape of the rings of Saturn was discovered by Christiaan Huygens, a Dutch astronomer, mathematician, and physicist. Huygens also developed the wave theory of light and made significant contributions to the science of dynamics and the use of the pendulum in clocks. His reputation in mathematics, as well as his wealth and parentage, enabled him to correspond with some of the leading scientists of his time, including René Descartes, Blaise Pascal, and Gottfried Wilhelm Leibniz. Late in life he met Isaac Newton, with whose theory of gravitation he disagreed.

Huygens was born in The Hague on April 14, 1629. He was trained by his father in languages and drawing, and at 13 began the study of mechanics. In 1645 he entered the University of Leiden to study mathematics and law. Two years later he transferred to the College of Breda.

At 21 Huygens published his first treatise on mathematics, following this with work on probability theory. At the same time he and his older brother discovered a new method of grinding and polishing lenses for use by astronomers. In 1655 he discovered Saturn's moon Titan. He identified the components of the Orion nebula in 1656 and, three years later, published his discoveries of the shape of Saturn's rings. His construction of a pendulum clock with an escapement aided in his observation of planetary motion.

Huygens lived in Paris from 1666 until 1681, when he returned to Holland. Written much earlier, his *Discourse on the Cause of Gravity* and *Treatise on Light* were published in 1690. He died on July 8, 1695, in The Hague.

CHAPTER 12

ISAAC NEWTON

T he chief figure of the scientific revolution of the 17th century was Sir Isaac Newton. He was a physicist and mathematician who laid the foundations of calculus and extended the understanding of color and light. He also studied the mechanics of planetary orbits, formulated three fundamental laws of motion, and developed the law of gravitation, thus founding what is now known as classical mechanics. His work established the commonly held scientific view of the world until Albert Einstein published his theories of relativity in the early 20th century.

Isaac Newton was born on Dec. 25, 1642, in Woolsthorpe, England. His father had died before he was born. Within a couple of years his mother remarried and sent him away to live with his grandmother. Newton was later sent to grammar school at Grantham to prepare for the university.

When Newton arrived at Trinity College, Cambridge, in 1661, he began studying the ancient teachings of Aristotle, as was then

Portrait of physicist and mathematician Isaac Newton. Hulton Archive/Getty Images

customary. Soon, however, he learned of the scientific revolution that had been going on in Europe through the work of Nicolaus Copernicus, Johannes Kepler, Galileo, and René Descartes. Newton became intrigued by the work of Descartes and other natural philosophers who, in contrast to Aristotle, viewed physical reality as composed entirely of particles of matter in motion. They held that all the phenomena of nature result from their mechanical interaction.

In 1665 Newton graduated and returned to Woolsthorpe. There he continued his study of light, gravity, and mathematics that ultimately led him to three of the greatest discoveries in the history of science.

Newton's experiments with light showed that white light passed through a prism broke up into a wide color band, called a spectrum. Passed through another prism, the color band became white light again. Next he passed a single color through a prism. It remained unchanged. From this he concluded that white light is a mixture of pure colors. He also formulated the corpuscular theory of light, which states that light is made up of tiny particles, or corpuscles, traveling in straight lines at great speeds.

An illustration that depicts Isaac Newton experimenting with light. A prism at the far right separates sunlight into it individual colors. A second prism turns the colored band back into white light. Robert Clifford Magis/National Geographic Image Collection/Getty Images

The law of gravitation arose from Newton questioning what keeps the Moon in its regular path around Earth. He concluded that an invisible force—gravity—acts between the two celestial bodies, and he formulated a mathematical expression for the gravitational force. It states that every object in the universe attracts every other object with a force that operates through empty space. This force varies with the masses of the objects and the distance between them.

In mathematics, Newton used the concepts of time and infinity to calculate the slopes of curves and the areas under curves. He developed his "fluxional" method—later known as calculus—in 1669 but did not publish it until 1704.

Meanwhile, Newton had been appointed professor of mathematics at Cambridge in 1669. Three years later he invented the reflecting telescope. In 1687 he completed his major work, *Principia* (*Philosophiae Naturalis Principia Mathematica,* or *Mathematical Principles of Natural Philosophy*). One of the fundamental works of modern science, it set forth the basic principles of classical mechanics concerning force, mass, and motion as well as the theory of gravitation.

Newton was elected to Parliament twice, as a representative of Cambridge. In 1696 he was appointed warden of the mint. At that time a complete recoinage and standardization of coins was taking place. When the project was completed in 1699, he was made master of the mint. He was elected president of the Royal Society in 1703 and was knighted in 1705. Newton died in London on March 20, 1727, and was the first scientist to be honored with burial in Westminster Abbey.

CHAPTER 13

EDMOND HALLEY

The English astronomer and mathematician Edmond Halley was the first to calculate the orbit of a comet later named after him. He also encouraged Isaac Newton to write his *Philosophiae Naturalis Principia Mathematica*, which Halley published in 1687 at his own expense.

Halley was born in Haggerston, Shoreditch, near London, on Nov. 8, 1656. He began his education at St. Paul's School, London, and in 1673 entered Queen's College at Oxford University. There he learned of John Flamsteed's project at the Royal Greenwich Observatory using the telescope to compile an accurate catalog of stars visible in the Northern Hemisphere. Halley proposed doing the same thing for the Southern Hemisphere. Leaving Oxford without his degree, he sailed for the island of St. Helena in the South Atlantic in 1676. His results were published in a star catalog in 1678, establishing the youth as a prominent astronomer.

Portrait of Edmond Halley. The Bridgeman Art Library/Getty Images

Halley, who sometimes spelled his first name Edmund, published the first meteorological chart in 1686 and the first magnetic charts of the Atlantic and Pacific areas, which were used in navigation for many years after his death. Continuing his work in observational astronomy, he published in 1705 *A Synopsis of the Astronomy of Comets*, in which he described 24 comets.

Halley's comet, the first comet whose return was predicted and, almost three centuries later, the first to be photographed up close by spacecraft. J. Lodriguss/Photo Researchers/Getty Images

Halley accurately predicted the return in 1758 of a comet—now known as Halley's comet—previously observed in 1531, 1607, and 1682. He died in Greenwich, on Jan. 14, 1742.

CHAPTER 14

WILLIAM HERSCHEL

The founder of modern stellar astronomy was a German-born organist, William Herschel. His discovery of Uranus in 1781 was the first identification of a planet since ancient times. Herschel developed theories of the structure of nebulas and the evolution of stars, cataloged many binary (or double) stars, and made significant modifications in the reflecting telescope. He also proved that the solar system moves through space and discovered infrared radiation.

Friedrich Wilhelm Herschel was born in Hannover, Germany, on Nov. 15, 1738. When he was 21 he moved to England to work as a musician; he later taught music, wrote symphonies, and conducted. He had made observations of the Sun at an early age but was 43 before he became a professional astronomer.

Herschel discovered Uranus with the first reflecting telescope that he built. The discovery brought him an appointment as astronomer for George III, and he was able to spend all his time studying the stars. He was knighted in 1816. Herschel's observations of binary stars—pairs of stars that appear close together in space—demonstrated that gravity governed the stars as well as the solar system. Herschel died in Slough, England, on Aug. 25, 1822.

CHAPTER 15

PIERRE-SIMON LAPLACE

O ne of the most brilliant astronomers in the history of the field was Frenchman Pierre-Simon Laplace. Using only mathematics, Laplace predicted many things that were later seen with powerful telescopes.

Laplace was born on March 23, 1749, in Beaumont-en-Auge, a village in Normandy. His father was poor, and Pierre-Simon received little early education. Wealthy neighbors took an interest in him, however, and sent him to the university at Caen. There he did very well in mathematics. At 18 he went to Paris with a letter explaining the principles of mechanics to give to Jean d'Alembert, a leading mathematician. D'Alembert was impressed, and he helped the young man get a position as professor of mathematics at the École Militaire.

In 1773 Laplace discovered the invariability of the planetary mean motions, meaning that changes in the orbits of the planets are small and short-lived. In other words, their orbits are regular and unchanging over the long term. This finding established the solar system's stability. Another important theory supporting stability was his discovery in 1787 of the dependence of the Moon's acceleration on the eccentricity of Earth's orbit.

With the mathematician Joseph-Louis Lagrange, Laplace reviewed the studies made since Isaac Newton's time on gravitational forces in the universe. Then he wrote *Celestial Mechanics*, issued in five volumes from 1798 to 1827. A condensed version contained his nebular hypothesis, a theory of the origin of the solar system. Laplace won many awards for his studies and was made a marquis, but he remained modest, saying, "What we know is little. What we know not is immense." He died in Paris on March 5, 1827.

CHAPTER 16

JOHN HERSCHEL

The English astronomer John Herschel made outstanding contributions in the observation and discovery of stars and nebulas. He was the son of noted astronomer Sir William Herschel.

John Frederick William Herschel was born in Slough, England, on March 7, 1792. In 1809 he entered the University of Cambridge, where he excelled in mathematics. In 1816 he began to assist his renowned father in astronomical research, gaining extensive experience in the construction and use of large telescopes. In 1820 he was among the founders of the Royal Astronomical Society.

Herschel's first major task in astronomy was the reobservation of the binary stars cataloged by his father. Working with James South between 1821 and 1823, he compiled a star catalog that earned the pair the Gold Medal of the Royal Astronomical Society. In 1833 Herschel completed and published the revision and extension of his father's catalogs.

Herschel's sense of obligation to complete his father's work led him to journey to the Southern Hemisphere to survey the skies not visible in England. Based near Cape Town in southern Africa, he spent four years (1834–38) recording the locations of 68,948 stars and compiling long catalogs of nebulas and binary, or double, stars. He also described many details of the Great Nebula in the constellation Orion, as well as the Magellanic Clouds—actually two galaxies visible only in the Southern Hemisphere—and observed Halley's comet and the satellites of Saturn.

Herschel was also a highly accomplished chemist. He invented a process of photography on sensitized paper and was the first to use the terms "positive" and "negative" in photography. In addition, he made important contributions to the physics of light and to mathematics. Herschel died on May 11, 1871, in Collingwood, England.

CHAPTER 17

KONSTANTIN TSIOLKOVSKY

One of the scientific dreamers who made the space age possible was Konstantin Tsiolkovsky. A Russian research scientist in aeronautics and astronautics, he pioneered rocket and space studies.

Tsiolkovsky was born in Izhevskoye in Russia's Ryazan Province on Sept. 17, 1857. Childhood scarlet fever left him deaf at age 9, and he became a lonely child devoted to his books. The years 1873 to 1876 he spent in Moscow studying mathematics and the physical sciences. He passed a teacher's examination after returning home and was assigned to a school in Borovsk. There, and at a later post in Kaluga, he pursued his scientific interests. To aid his research into the aerodynamics of airfoils, he built a succession of wind tunnels, mostly at his own expense. These wind tunnels, the first in Russia, permitted the testing of various aircraft designs.

During his research, Tsiolkovsky began to devote more attention to space problems, even showing an interest in life on other planets. His book *Dreams of Earth and Sky* was published in 1895. In 1896 he began work on *Exploration of Cosmic Space by Means of Reaction Devices*, which dealt with theoretical problems of using rocket engines in space and other related problems.

The years from 1901 to 1915 were filled with sadness and frustration. A son committed suicide in 1902, a flood swept away much of his research in 1908, and a daughter was arrested for revolutionary activity in 1911. In addition, Russian scientific authorities were indifferent to his work.

But in the final 18 years of his life, after the Russian Revolution of 1917, Tsiolkovsky was able to continue his work with the support of the new Soviet government. His work on stratospheric exploration and interplanetary flight played a significant role in modern astronautics. He was elected to the Academy of Sciences in 1919 and was granted a pension for life in 1921 in recognition for his services in education and aviation. He died in Kaluga on Sept. 19, 1935.

CHAPTER 18

ROBERT H. GODDARD

In fiction the space age began in the novels of such writers as H.G. Wells, author of *The Time Machine* and other books, and in the comic strips of "Buck Rogers" and "Flash Gordon." In real life the age of space exploration was quietly ushered in by the publication of *A Method of Reaching Extreme Altitudes* by U.S. physicist Robert Hutchings Goddard in 1919. Goddard pioneered the development of rockets that used fuels such as liquid oxygen and liquid hydrogen.

Goddard was born in Worcester, Mass., on Oct. 5, 1882. His childhood interest in things mechanical was greatly heightened in 1898 with the publication of the novel *War of the Worlds* by H.G. Wells. He was to spend the rest of his life dreaming about, and working for, the construction of a spaceflight machine.

Goddard attended Worcester Polytechnic Institute and in 1908 began a long association with Clark University in Worcester, where he earned his doctorate,

Physicist Robert Goddard, the father of modern rocketry, posing with the framework supporting a rocket (top) *prior to launch.* Hulton Archive/Archive Photos/Getty Images

taught physics, and carried out rocket experiments. In a laboratory test in 1925 a liquid-fueled rocket operated satisfactorily, and on March 16, 1926, the world's first flight of a liquid-fueled rocket took place on a farm near Auburn, Mass., achieving a brief lift-off.

Over the years Goddard's experiments and research were supported and financed by help from the Smithsonian Institution, Charles A. Lindbergh, and philanthropist Harry F. Guggenheim. From 1930 until the mid-1940s, Goddard and associates did their experiments at Roswell, N.M. He spent the time in the search for an adequate high-altitude rocket. In 1935 he became the first man to shoot a liquid-fueled rocket faster than the speed of sound. He obtained patents for a steering apparatus for rocket machines, developed staged rockets to reach great altitudes, and made rocket fuel pumps, a self-cooling rocket motor, and other components.

Although Goddard was ridiculed by the public and the press in his lifetime, when he died in Baltimore, Md., on Aug. 10, 1945, the world was on the verge of the jet and rocket ages. Since that time he has been acknowledged as the father of modern rocketry.

CHAPTER 19

EDWIN POWELL HUBBLE

A U.S. astronomer, Edwin Powell Hubble played a crucial role in establishing the field of extragalactic astronomy—the study of objects outside the Milky Way galaxy. He is generally regarded as the leading astronomer of the 20th century.

Hubble was born in Marshfield, Mo., on Nov. 20, 1889. In 1910 he graduated from the University of Chicago and was selected as a Rhodes Scholar. He spent three years at the University of Oxford and was awarded a B.A. in jurisprudence, a subject he had taken at the insistence of his father. After his father's death in 1913, the way was open for him to pursue a scientific career. He returned to the United States and began graduate studies in astronomy at the University of Chicago.

After serving in the U.S. Army during World War I, Hubble earned his doctorate and went to work with his former teacher, George Hale, at the Mount Wilson Observatory in California. There

U.S. astronomer Edwin Powell Hubble, posing at his desk. Hubble helped proved that the universe includes many different galaxies outside of the Milky Way. © Huntington Library/ SuperStock

he observed spiral nebulas, objects he had investigated for his doctorate. At the time it was unclear whether these objects were distant star systems comparable to the Milky Way galaxy or clouds of gas or sparse star clusters within, or close by, the Milky Way.

In 1923 Hubble found a type of star called Cepheid variables in the Andromeda Nebula, a very well-known spiral. He used the fluctuations in light of these stars to determine the nebula's distance. He determined that the nebula was several hundred thousand light-years away (outside the Milky Way galaxy) and that it was actually another galaxy. Hubble's finds in the Andromeda Nebula and other relatively nearby spiral nebulae swiftly convinced the great majority of astronomers that the universe in fact contains many galaxies.

In studying those galaxies, Hubble made his second remarkable discovery in 1927,

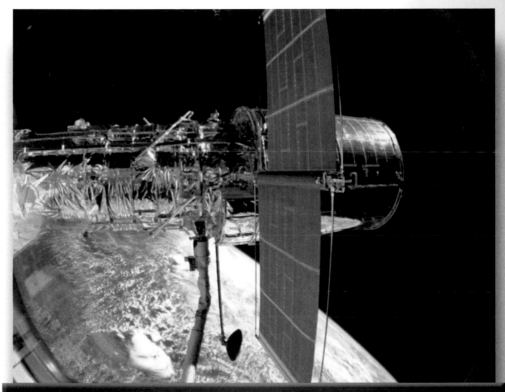

A color image of the Hubble Space Telescope, named for Edwin Hubble. Jupiterimages/ Photos.com/Thinkstock

that galaxies were receding from the Milky Way at rates that increased with distance. This implied that the universe, long considered unchanging, was expanding. Even more remarkable, the ratio of the galaxies' speed to their distance was a constant, named Hubble's constant in his honor. Hubble's original calculation of the constant was incorrect; it made the Milky Way larger than all other galaxies and the entire universe younger than the surmised age of Earth. Later astronomers determined that galaxies were systematically more distant, resolving the discrepancy.

Hubble died in San Marino, Calif., on Sept. 28, 1953. The Hubble Space Telescope was named after him.

CHAPTER 20

HERMANN OBERTH

The German mathematician and physicist Hermann Oberth made many advances in rocket science. Along with Robert H. Goddard of the United States and Konstantin Tsiolkovsky of Russia, Oberth is generally credited as one of the founders of modern astronautics. Unlike the others, however, he lived to see space travel become a reality.

Hermann Julius Oberth was born on June 25, 1894, in Nagyszeben, Austria-Hungary (now Sibiu, Romania). After leaving military service in World War I, he studied at the University of Heidelberg, Germany. In 1923 he published a book, based on his university dissertation, that aroused public interest in space travel, even though the university had denied him a degree. The book explained how a liquid-fueled rocket could be made to go fast enough to enter space.

In 1930 Oberth patented a liquid-fueled rocket, which he later built and tested. One of his assistants was the young rocket scientist Werner von Braun. In 1938 Oberth joined the faculty of the Technical University of Vienna, Austria. He became a German citizen in 1940 and went to work for Braun at the rocket center in Peenemünde, Germany, in 1941. In 1943 he began work on solid-fueled rockets.

After the end of World War II Oberth worked in West Germany, Switzerland, and Italy. In 1954 he published a book about space travel that was later translated into English as *Man into Space*. In 1955 he rejoined Braun at the U.S. Army's Redstone Arsenal in Huntsville, Ala. In 1958 he returned to Germany, and in 1962 he retired. He died on Dec. 29, 1989, in Nürnberg, West Germany.

CHAPTER 21

JAN HENDRIK OORT

The Dutch astronomer Jan Hendrik Oort was one of the most important figures in 20th-century efforts to understand the nature of the Milky Way galaxy. The Oort cloud, an enormous cloud of comets surrounding the solar system, was named for him.

Oort was born in Franeker, Netherlands, on April 28, 1900. After studies at the University of Groningen, he was appointed astronomer to the Leiden Observatory in 1924 and became director in 1945, a position he held until 1970. In 1925 Bertil Lindblad of Sweden had advanced the theory that the Milky Way rotates in its own plane around the center of the galaxy. Oort was able to confirm this theory in 1927 through his own observations of star velocities in the galaxy. He modified the theory substantially into the form used thereafter.

Oort's subsequent work, as well as that of the school of astronomy he developed in the Netherlands, was directed toward strengthening and testing the Lindblad-Oort theory. Soon after becoming a professor at the University of Leiden in 1935, he determined that the Sun is 30,000 light-years from the center of the galaxy and takes 225 million years to complete an orbit around it.

In 1950 Oort proposed that comets originate from a vast cloud of small bodies that orbit the Sun at a distance of about one light-year. Further, he stated that the approach of other stars toward this cloud alters some comets' orbits so that they pass close to the Sun. The existence of this region, which was named the Oort Cloud, eventually came to be accepted by most astronomers.

From 1958 to 1961 Oort was president of the International Astronomical Union, of which he had been general secretary from 1935 to 1948. He died in Leiden on Nov. 5, 1992.

CHAPTER 22

GERARD PETER KUIPER

A Dutch-American astronomer, Gerard Peter Kuiper is known for his discoveries and theories concerning the solar system. Among his many other ideas, he suggested the existence of a disk-shaped belt of comets orbiting the Sun beyond the orbit of the planet Neptune. The existence of this belt of millions of comets was verified in the 1990s, and it was named the Kuiper belt in his honor.

Gerrit Pieter Kuiper was born on Dec. 7, 1905, in Harenkarspel, Netherlands. He graduated from the University of Leiden in 1927 and received his Ph.D. from that school in 1933. That same year he moved to the United States, where he became a naturalized citizen in 1937. He joined the staff of Yerkes Observatory of the University of Chicago in 1936, twice serving as director (1947–49 and 1957–60) of both Yerkes and McDonald observatories. Kuiper founded the Lunar and Planetary Laboratory at the University of Arizona

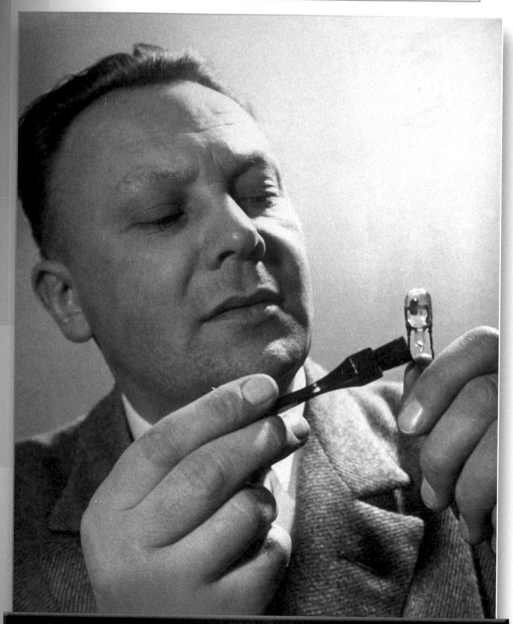

Astronomer Gerard Peter Kuiper, inspecting a spectrometer tube. He suggested the existence of a disk-shaped belt of comets now known as the Kuiper belt. Cornell Capa/Time & Life Pictures/Getty Images

in 1960 and served as its director until his death in 1973.

After conducting research in stellar astronomy, Kuiper shifted his focus to planetary research in the 1940s. In 1944 he was able to confirm the presence of a methane atmosphere around Saturn's moon Titan. In 1947 he predicted (correctly) that carbon dioxide is a major component of the atmosphere of Mars, and he also correctly predicted that the rings of Saturn are composed of particles of ice. That same year he discovered the fifth moon of Uranus (Miranda), and in 1949 he discovered the second moon of Neptune (Nereid). Also in 1949 he proposed an influential theory of the origin of the solar system, suggesting that the planets had formed by the condensation of a large cloud of gas around the Sun.

In 1950 Kuiper obtained the first reliable measurement of the visual diameter of Pluto. In 1956 he proved that Mars's polar ice caps are composed of frozen water, not of carbon dioxide as had been previously assumed. Kuiper's 1964 prediction of what the surface of the Moon would be like to walk on ("it would be like crunchy snow") was verified by the astronaut Neil Armstrong in 1969.

Kuiper died on Dec. 23, 1973, in Mexico City, Mexico. The Kuiper Airborne Observatory (1974) was named after him, as were craters on the Moon, Mercury, and Mars.

CHAPTER 23

WERNHER VON BRAUN

A German-born engineer, Wernher von Braun played a prominent role in all aspects of rocketry and space exploration. He was well known for his work in both Germany and the United States.

Braun was born in Wirsitz, Germany, on March 23, 1912. He graduated from the Berlin Institute of Technology in 1932 with a degree in mechanical engineering, and entered the University of Berlin. Two years later he received a Ph.D. in physics. During World War II he was technical director of rocket research and production in Peenemünde, Germany. The V-2 rocket, used to bomb London, was developed there.

At the end of the war, Braun and his entire rocket development team surrendered to U.S. troops. He settled in Huntsville, Ala., in 1952 and became technical director, and later chief, of the U.S. Army ballistic weapon program. On Jan. 31, 1958, Braun and his Army group launched the first U.S. Earth satellite, Explorer 1.

Wernher von Braun, 1962. NASA; photograph, © Fabian Bachrach

As director of the George C. Marshall Space Flight Center in Huntsville, Braun led the development of the large and extremely complex space launch vehicles Saturn I, IB, and V. In 1975 he founded the National Space Institute, a private organization whose objective was to gain public support and understanding of space activities. Braun received numerous awards for his work. He died in Alexandria, Va., on June 16, 1977.

CHAPTER 24

JAMES A. VAN ALLEN

One of the major discoveries made by space probes in 1958 was information leading to the discovery of two huge, doughnut-shaped belts of intense radiation encircling Earth. The inner belt is made up of high-energy protons, the outer belt of high-energy electrons and other particles. The belts are part of the magnetosphere, the tear-shaped magnetic region around Earth. The bands start at an altitude of several hundred miles from Earth and extend for several thousand miles into space. These radiation belts were named for James A. Van Allen, whose work helped bring about their discovery.

James Alfred Van Allen was born on Sept. 7, 1914, in Mount Pleasant, Iowa. His father was an attorney. A studious boy with a great interest in science, Van Allen entered Iowa Wesleyan College, where, in 1931, he studied physics and chemistry. After receiving a bachelor of science degree there, he was awarded a master's degree and a doctorate from the

University of Iowa. From 1939 to 1942 he was a research scientist at the Carnegie Institution in Washington, D.C. During part of World War II Van Allen served as a naval officer; he helped develop the radio equipment for naval artillery shells.

After the war Van Allen was made head of high-altitude research at the Applied Physics Laboratory of Johns Hopkins University. There he worked with captured German V-2 rockets and led in the design of the Aerobee, one of the first U.S.-built rockets used for upper atmosphere exploration.

Van Allen returned to the University of Iowa in 1951 and was named chairman of the physics department. There he conducted many cosmic-ray studies. He launched his rockets from balloons positioned 10 to 15 miles (16 to 24 kilometers) up in the atmosphere. Van Allen was one of the scientists who proposed a program of worldwide cooperation in research, the International Geophysical Year (IGY) of 1957–58. He designed and built the instrument payloads for the U.S. satellites launched under the IGY. These satellites sent radio reports on outer space conditions back to listening stations on Earth.

On Jan. 31, 1958, the first U.S. Earth satellite, Explorer 1, went into orbit, equipped with Van Allen instruments. These instruments detected two radiation belts. Later Explorer satellites also carried Van Allen instruments, as did the Pioneer series of Moon probes.

Van Allen later participated in the development of numerous space probes built to study planetary and solar physics. He was elected to the National Academy of Sciences in 1959 and became president of the American Geophysical Union in 1982. He died in Iowa City, Iowa, on Aug. 9, 2006.

CHAPTER 25

JOHN H. GLENN, JR.

Astronaut John H. Glenn, Jr., made history in 1962 when he became the first American to orbit Earth. He later had a long career in politics.

John Herschel Glenn, Jr., was born in Cambridge, Ohio. As a Marine fighter pilot in World War II and the Korean War, Glenn flew 149 missions, withstanding 11 hits by enemy fire. Following the Korean War, he served as a test pilot for several years, working with Navy and Marine Corps jet fighters and attack aircraft. In 1957 Glenn set a transcontinental speed record from Los Angeles to New York.

In 1959 Glenn was selected as one of the Mercury Seven—the first seven astronauts in the U.S. space travel program. On Feb. 20, 1962, he entered the space capsule Friendship 7 and began his historic mission, orbiting Earth three times within a five-hour period. The success of the mission instantly boosted American morale, which had lagged during the Cold War years because of the lead the Soviet Union had taken in the space race. Upon his return to Earth, Glenn was hailed as a genuine American hero and was honored with a ticker-tape parade down Broadway in New York City. He also received the Space Congressional Medal of Honor.

Glenn resigned from the space program in 1964 and from the Marine Corps in 1965. He then pursued a political career and was elected to the U.S. Senate from Ohio in 1974. However, Senator Glenn never lost his interest in the phenomenon of space flight, and he became instrumental in promoting the use of space flight for the benefit of healthy and productive aging.

In October 1998 Glenn returned to space as a payload specialist on a nine-day mission aboard the space shuttle *Discovery*. At age 77, he was the oldest person ever to travel in space. During the mission he participated in experiments that studied similarities between the aging process and the body's response to weightlessness.

CHAPTER 26

ALAN B. SHEPARD, JR.

The first U.S. astronaut to travel in space was Alan B. Shepard, Jr. His historic flight in 1961 energized U.S. space efforts and made him a national hero.

Alan Bartlett Shepard, Jr., was born on Nov. 18, 1923, in East Derry, N.H. He graduated from the U.S. Naval Academy in Annapolis, Md., in 1944 and served in the Pacific during World War II on board the destroyer *Cogswell*. He earned his naval aviator wings in 1947, qualified as a test pilot in 1951, and experimented with high-altitude aircraft, in-flight fueling systems, and landings on angled carrier decks. In 1957 he graduated from the Naval War College in Newport, R.I.

In 1959 Shepard became one of the original seven astronauts chosen for the U.S. Mercury program by the National Aeronautics and Space Administration (NASA). On May 5, 1961, he made a 15-minute suborbital flight in the Freedom 7 spacecraft, which reached an altitude of

115 miles (185 kilometers). The flight came 23 days after Soviet cosmonaut Yury Gagarin became the first human to travel in space.

Shepard was selected as command pilot for the first manned Gemini mission, Gemini 3, but he was grounded in 1964 because of Ménière disease, an ailment that affects the inner ear. In 1969 he underwent corrective surgery that allowed him to return to full flight status.

Apollo 14 astronaut Alan B. Shepard, Jr., standing by the U.S. flag on the Moon, Feb. 5, 1971. Johnson Space Center/NASA

Shepard commanded the Apollo 14 flight (Jan. 31–Feb. 9, 1971; with Stuart A. Roosa and Edgar D. Mitchell), which involved the first landing in the Moon's Fra Mauro highlands. Near the end of his Moon walk, Shepard—an avid golfer—swung at two golf balls with a makeshift six-iron club as a playful demonstration for live television cameras of the weak lunar gravity.

Shepard headed NASA's astronaut office from 1963 to 1969 and from 1971 to 1974. Following his second tenure he retired from the Navy as a rear admiral and from the space program to undertake a career in private business in Texas. He received numerous awards, including the NASA Distinguished Service Medal and the Congressional Medal of Honor. He also coauthored, with fellow Mercury astronaut Deke Slayton, *Moon Shot: The Inside Story of America's Race to the Moon* (1994). Shepard died in Monterey, Calif., on July 21, 1998.

CHAPTER 27

BUZZ ALDRIN

U.S. astronaut Edwin E. Aldrin, Jr., was the second man to set foot on the Moon. He is better known by his lifelong nickname, Buzz.

Edwin Eugene Aldrin, Jr., was born in Montclair, N.J., on Jan. 20, 1930. After graduating from the U.S. Military Academy in West Point, N.Y., in 1951 he became an Air Force pilot. He flew 66 combat missions in Korea and later served in West Germany. In 1963 he wrote a dissertation on orbital mechanics to earn a Ph.D. from the Massachusetts Institute of Technology. Later that year he was chosen as an astronaut.

On Nov. 11, 1966, Aldrin joined James A. Lovell, Jr., on the four-day Gemini 12 flight. Aldrin's record 5½-hour walk in space proved that humans can function effectively in the vacuum of space.

Apollo 11, manned by Aldrin, Neil A. Armstrong, and Michael Collins, was launched to the Moon on July 16, 1969. Four days later Armstrong and Aldrin landed the lunar module Eagle near the edge of Mare Tranquillitatis. The Eagle stood on the Moon for 21 hours and 37 minutes, during which the astronauts spent more than two hours on the surface gathering rock samples, taking photographs, and setting up scientific equipment while millions watched on television. Armstrong and Aldrin later piloted the Eagle to a successful rendezvous

Astronaut Edwin ("Buzz") Aldrin, Jr., pilot of the Gemini 12 spacecraft, practicing extravehicular work during underwater zero-gravity training. NASA Johnson Space Center Collection

Apollo 11 astronaut Buzz Aldrin, photographed on July 20, 1969, during the first manned mission to the Moon's surface. Reflected in Aldrin's faceplate is the Lunar Module and astronaut Neil Armstrong, who took the picture. NASA

with Collins and the command module in lunar orbit. The mission ended on July 24 with splashdown in the Pacific Ocean.

Aldrin retired from the National Aeronautics and Space Administration in 1971 to become commandant of the Aerospace Research Pilot School at Edwards Air Force Base in California. In 1972 he retired from the Air Force to enter private business. In 1988 he legally changed his name to Buzz Aldrin.

In 1998 Aldrin founded the ShareSpace Foundation, a nonprofit organization to promote the expansion of manned space travel. He wrote two autobiographies, *Return to Earth* (1973) and *Magnificent Desolation: The Long Journey Home from the Moon* (2009, with Ken Abraham). He also wrote a history of the Apollo program, *Men from Earth* (1989, with Malcolm McConnell), and two children's books, *Reaching for the Moon* (2005) and *Look to the Stars* (2009).

CHAPTER 28

NEIL ARMSTRONG

The first person to set foot on the Moon was U.S. astronaut Neil Armstrong. As he stepped onto the Moon's dusty surface, he spoke the now famous words, "That's one small step for [a] man, one giant leap for mankind."

Born in Wapakoneta, Ohio, on Aug. 5, 1930, Neil Alden Armstrong knew early in life that he wanted an aviation career. On his 16th birthday he became a licensed pilot; a year later, in 1947, he was a naval air cadet. After studying aeronautical engineering and serving in the Korean War, he became a civilian research pilot for the National Advisory Committee for Aeronautics, later known as the National Aeronautics and Space Administration (NASA) in 1955.

Armstrong joined NASA's space program in 1962. On March 16, 1966, as command pilot of the Gemini 8 spacecraft, he and David R. Scott docked with an unmanned Agena rocket, thus completing the first manual space-docking maneuver.

U.S. astronaut Neil Armstrong, preparing for the launch of Gemini 8 in 1966. Armstrong is perhaps best known as the first person to set foot on the Moon. NASA

On July 16, 1969, Armstrong, along with Buzz Aldrin and Michael Collins, blasted off on the Apollo 11 mission to land men on the Moon. On July 20 the Eagle lunar module, with Armstrong and Aldrin aboard, separated from the command module and, guided manually by Armstrong, touched down. During their more than 21 hours on the Moon, the astronauts spent about two hours walking on the surface collecting soil and rock samples, taking photographs, and deploying scientific instruments. The voyage back to Earth began on July 21, and the trio splashed down in the Pacific Ocean on July 24.

Armstrong resigned from NASA in 1971. From then until 1979 he was professor of aerospace engineering at the University of Cincinnati in Ohio. After 1979 Armstrong served as chairman or director for a number of companies, among them Computing Technologies for Aviation, from 1982 to 1992, and AIL Systems (later EDO Corporation), a maker of electronic equipment for the military, from 1977 until his retirement in 2002.

CHAPTER 29

JOHN W. YOUNG

U.S. astronaut John W. Young participated in the Gemini, Apollo, and space shuttle programs. He was the first astronaut to make five—and later the first to make six—spaceflights. In 1965 he served as Virgil I. Grissom's copilot on Gemini 3, the first U.S. two-man spaceflight.

John Watts Young was born on Sept. 24, 1930, in San Francisco, Calif. After graduating from Georgia Institute of Technology in 1952 with a degree in aeronautical engineering, he joined the U.S. Navy. He served in Korea before participating in a test project during which, in 1962, he set two time-to-climb records in an F-4B Navy jet. From 1962 to 1964 Young trained for his part in the National Aeronautics and Space Administration (NASA) project.

Gemini 3, launched on March 23, 1965, reached a maximum altitude of 139 miles (224 kilometers) on the initial orbit. The orbit was changed three times, and after

4 hours 53 minutes flight time, the space-craft landed in the South Atlantic Ocean. On July 18, 1966, Young joined Michael Collins on the Gemini 10 flight. The two docked with an Agena target vehicle and, using the Agena's engine, attained an altitude of 475 miles (764 kilometers).

On May 18, 1969, Apollo 10 was launched, with Thomas P. Stafford, Eugene A. Cernan, and Young on board. The flight, which orbited the Moon, was the last checkout of Apollo systems before the Moon landing of Apollo 11. Young was commander of the Apollo 16 mission (April 16–27, 1972; with Charles M. Duke, Jr., and Thomas K. Mattingly), the fifth manned landing on the Moon. He retired from the Navy in 1976 but remained with the space program, becoming chief of the astronaut office.

Young was commander of the first space shuttle mission (April 12–14, 1981; with Robert L. Crippen), guiding the orbiter *Columbia* to a landing at Edwards Air Force Base in California after it had circled Earth 36 times. In 1983 Young commanded the joint NASA and European Space Agency mission, which from November 28 to

December 8 carried Spacelab, a scientific workshop, in *Columbia*'s payload bay. Beginning in 1987 he held management positions concerned with space shuttle operations and safety at the Johnson Space Center in Houston, Texas. Young retired from NASA in 2004.

CHAPTER 30

MICHAEL COLLINS

U.S. astronaut Michael Collins was the command module pilot of Apollo 11, the first manned Moon landing mission. He orbited above the Moon while Neil Armstrong and Buzz Aldrin walked on its surface.

Michael Collins, 1969. NASA/Johnson Space Center

Collins was born in Rome, Italy, on Oct. 31, 1930. A graduate of the U.S. Military Academy at West Point, N.Y., he transferred to the Air Force, becoming a test pilot at Edwards Air Force Base in California. He joined the space program in 1963.

Gemini 10, manned by Collins and command pilot John W. Young, was launched on July 18, 1966. After a rendezvous with an Agena target vehicle, the two men used the Agena's engines to propel them to a record altitude of 475 miles (764 kilometers). Collins left the spacecraft to remove equipment needed for an experiment from the Gemini and tried unsuccessfully to attach similar equipment to the Agena. He succeeded in retrieving an instrument from the Agena, but his activity was cut short because the Gemini craft was low on fuel. Gemini 10 returned to Earth on July 21.

On July 16, 1969, Collins was launched to the Moon in the Apollo 11 mission with commander Neil A. Armstrong and lunar module pilot Buzz Aldrin. Armstrong and Aldrin landed on the Moon in the lunar module Eagle on July 20 while Collins remained in the command module Columbia, circling the Moon at an altitude of 60–75 miles (97–121 kilometers). On July 21 Armstrong and Aldrin rejoined him, and the following day the astronauts left lunar orbit. They splashed down in the Pacific Ocean on July 24.

Apollo 11 was Collins's last space mission. Later in 1969 he was appointed assistant secretary of state for public affairs. In 1971 he became the first director of the National

Air and Space Museum in Washington, D.C.; in 1978 he became undersecretary of the Smithsonian Institution. From 1980 to 1985 he was vice president for field operations for Vought Corporation, an American aerospace firm. Collins also wrote several books, including an account of the Apollo 11 mission, *Carrying the Fire* (1974), and a history of the American space program, *Liftoff* (1988).

CHAPTER 31

EDWARD H. WHITE II

E dward H. White II was the first U.S. astronaut to walk in space. White made his space walk during the Gemini 4 mission in 1965.

Edward Higgins White II was born in San Antonio, Tex., on Nov. 14, 1930. He graduated from the U.S. Military Academy in West Point, N.Y., in 1952 and was commissioned a second lieutenant in the U.S. Air Force. He took flight training and served in a fighter squadron in Germany. In 1959 he received a master's degree in aeronautical engineering from the University of Michigan, Ann Arbor, and graduated from the Air Force Test Pilot School at Edwards Air Force Base in California.

Gemini 4 astronaut Edward White during his historic 21-minute space walk on June 5, 1965. NASA

White was selected in 1962 as a member of the second group of astronauts. Often called the most physically fit astronaut, he was chosen to join James A. McDivitt on the four-day orbital flight of Gemini 4, launched on June 3, 1965. During the third orbit White emerged from the spacecraft, secured by a 25-foot (7.6-meter) umbilical and tether line. He became the first person to propel himself in space with a maneuvering unit, floating in space for about 20 minutes.

White was subsequently one of the three-man crew of Apollo 1, who were the first casualties of the U.S. space program. The trio were killed during a flight simulation at Cape Kennedy, Fla., on Jan. 27, 1967.

CHAPTER 32

YURY GAGARIN

The world's first astronaut was a 27-year-old Soviet aviator named Yury Gagarin. On April 12, 1961, the 4.75-ton spacecraft Vostok 1 was launched at 9:07 in the morning, Moscow time, from a location in Baikonur, a wasteland in the south-central region of the Soviet Union (now in Kazakhstan). The spacecraft orbited Earth once in 1 hour and 29 minutes at a maximum speed of 17,000 miles (27,000 kilometers) per hour. It followed an elliptical orbit that carried Gagarin as far as 187 miles (301 kilometers) from Earth. Vostok 1 landed at 10:55 AM, making the young Soviet cosmonaut a worldwide celebrity.

Yury Alekseyevich Gagarin was born on March 9, 1934, on a collective farm near Gzhatsk, about 100 miles (160 kilometers) west of Moscow. His early education was interrupted by World War II. After his early schooling, he attended a vocational school at Lyubertsy, a Moscow suburb. It was here that he first became interested in

Soviet cosmonaut Yury Gagarin, preparing for launch aboard Vostok 1 in 1961. Gagarin was the first person to travel into outer space. Rolls Press/Popperfoto/Getty Images

flight. Following graduation in 1951, Gagarin attended the industrial college at Saratov, where he learned to fly. After graduation in 1955 he became a Soviet air force cadet. He completed his flight training in 1957 and joined the air force. After two years as a test pilot he was admitted to the astronaut training program.

Gagarin's flight in Vostok 1 was an astounding achievement that began humankind's entry into space. It was recognized that the Soviet Union had a definite advantage in space technology over the United States. It was his achievement that prompted the United States to launch its program to get a man on the Moon by the end of the 1960s.

Gagarin was celebrated as a hero in the Soviet Union. Monuments were raised to him and streets named in his honor. He never went into space again. He resumed his test flight career and was killed on March 27, 1968, on a routine mission near Moscow.

CHAPTER 33

ALEKSEY ARKHIPOVICH LEONOV

The Soviet cosmonaut Aleksey Arkhipovich Leonov performed the first space walk in history. Leonov maneuvered in space for 10 minutes after exiting the Voskhod 2 spacecraft in 1965.

Leonov was born on May 30, 1934, near Kemerovo, Russian S.F.S.R. After early schooling in Kaliningrad, he joined the Soviet air force in 1953. He completed his flight training in 1957 and served as a fighter pilot until 1959, when he was selected for cosmonaut training.

On March 18, 1965, Voskhod 2 was launched into space with Leonov and Pavel Belyayev aboard. During the second orbit Leonov let himself out of the spacecraft by means of an air lock while about 110 miles (177 kilometers) above the Crimea. Tethered to the ship, Leonov made observations, took motion pictures, and practiced maneuvering in free-fall for about 10 minutes before reentering Voskhod 2 over western Siberia. The ship landed after completing 17 orbits (26 hours) in space.

A decade later, Leonov was commander of the Soyuz 19 craft that linked in orbit with the U.S. Apollo craft on July 17, 1975, for the first joint Soviet-American space-flight. He retired as a cosmonaut in 1982; from then until 1991 he worked at the Yury Gagarin Cosmonaut Training Centre in Star City, near Moscow. In 2004 he wrote a book, *Two Sides of the Moon: Our Story of the Cold War Space Race*, with U.S. astronaut David Scott.

CHAPTER 34

VALENTINA TERESHKOVA

The first woman to travel in space was a Soviet cosmonaut named Valentina Tereshkova. Her spacecraft, Vostok 6, was launched on June 16, 1963. It completed 48 orbits of Earth in 71 hours before landing safely. In space at the same time was fellow cosmonaut Valeri F. Bykovsky, who had been launched two days earlier in Vostok 5. His craft also landed on June 19.

Tereshkova was born on March 6, 1937, in Maslennikovo, Russian S.F.S.R., near the larger city of Yaroslavl. Because her father was killed early in World War II, her early life was difficult. She did not begin schooling until age 10, and by age 17 she was an apprentice at the Yaroslavl tire factory. She became an ardent communist, joined the Komsomol (Communist Youth League), and took up parachuting as a hobby. Her work in the Komsomol and her devotion and expertise in parachute jumping helped her win a chance at being a cosmonaut.

The first woman launched into space, cosmonaut Valentina Tereshkova, seen wishing people a happy new year on Soviet television in 1966. Gamma-Keystone via Getty Images

In 1961 she became a member of the Communist Party.

That same year Yury Gagarin had become the first person to orbit Earth. Inspired by his feat, Tereshkova applied to become a cosmonaut. In spite of the fact that she had no training as a pilot, she was accepted for the Soviet space program in 1962.

After her flight she left the space program and married cosmonaut Andriyan G. Nikolayev. She also became an active and powerful member of the Supreme Soviet. In 1968 Tereshkova was chosen to head the Soviet Women's Committee. From 1974 to 1991 she served as a member of the Supreme Soviet Presidium. She was twice awarded the Order of Lenin, the highest civilian award of the Soviet Union. In 2008 she was elected to the State Duma, the lower house of the Russian legislature.

CHAPTER 35

ROBERT LAUREL CRIPPEN

Astronaut Robert Laurel Crippen served as pilot on the first U.S. space shuttle orbital flight. He later commanded several other shuttle missions.

Born on Sept. 11, 1937, in Beaumont, Tex., Crippen graduated from the University of Texas, Austin, in 1960 with a degree in aerospace engineering. He entered the U.S. Air Force Manned Orbiting Laboratory program in 1966 and transferred to the astronaut corps in 1969. He was named commander of the Skylab Medical Experiments Altitude Test several years later and was a member of the support crews for Skylab 2, 3, and 4, as well as the Apollo-Soyuz Test Project.

Manned by Crippen and John W. Young, the

Robert Laurel Crippen, 1984. NASA/Johnson Space Center

shuttle *Columbia*, the world's first reusable spacecraft, was launched on April 12, 1981. The two astronauts landed the airplanelike craft on April 14, after having orbited Earth 36 times. Crippen later commanded the second flight of the space shuttle *Challenger*. This flight (June 18–24, 1983) saw the first American woman in space, Sally Ride, and made Crippen the first to fly in two shuttle missions.

In 1984 he commanded two more shuttle flights. STS-41-C (*Challenger*, April 6–13, 1984) was the first mission in which a satellite, the malfunctioning Solar Maximum Mission, was repaired in Earth orbit. He then commanded STS-41-G (*Challenger*, Oct. 5–13, 1984), which was the first spaceflight with a seven-person crew and during which astronaut Kathryn Sullivan became the first American woman to walk in space.

From 1990 to 1992 Crippen was director of the space shuttle program, and from 1992 to 1995 he was director of the Kennedy Space Center in Florida. He served as president of a Utah aerospace firm from 1996 to 2001.

CHAPTER 36

CHRISTA CORRIGAN McAULIFFE

A n American teacher, Christa Corrigan McAuliffe was chosen to be the first private citizen in space. The death of McAuliffe and her fellow crew members in the 1986 space shuttle *Challenger* disaster was deeply felt by the country and had a strong effect on the U.S. space program.

Sharon Christa Corrigan was born on Sept. 2, 1948, in Boston, Mass. She earned her B.A. from Framingham (Massachusetts) State College in 1970 and the same year married Steve McAuliffe. Also in that year, she began a teaching career that impressed both her colleagues and her students with her energy and dedication. She received her master's degree in education from Bowie (Maryland) State College (now University) in 1978.

In 1984 McAuliffe was selected from among some 10,000 applications to be the first nonscientist in space. In her application she proposed keeping a three-part journal of her experiences: the first

Teacher Christa Corrigan McAullife, scheduled to be the first private citizen in space, experiencing zero gravity in a specially designed National Aeronautics and Space Administration (NASA) aircraft. NASA

part describing the training she would go through, the second chronicling the details of the actual flight, and the third relating her feelings and experiences back on Earth. She also planned to keep a video record of her activities. McAuliffe was to conduct at least two lessons while on board the space shuttle to be simulcast to students around the world, and she was to spend the nine months following her return home lecturing to students across the United States.

The space shuttle Challenger *exploding and breaking apart shortly after liftoff on Jan. 28, 1986.* NASA

Problems dogged the ill-fated *Challenger* mission from the start. The launch had been postponed for several days, and the night before the launch, central Florida was hit by a severe cold front that left ice on the launchpad. The shuttle finally was launched at 11:38 AM on Jan. 28, 1986. Just 73 seconds after liftoff the craft exploded, sending debris cascading into the Atlantic Ocean for more than an hour afterward. There were no survivors. The live television coverage of the spectacular and tragic event, coupled with McAuliffe's winning, dynamic, and (not least) civilian presence on board, halted shuttle missions for two and a half years, sorely damaged the reputation of the National Aeronautics and Space Administration (NASA), and eroded public support for the space program.

CHAPTER 37

SALLY RIDE

The first American woman to travel into outer space was the astronaut Sally Ride. Only two other women preceded her: Valentina Tereshkova (1963) and Svetlana Savitskaya (1982), both from the former Soviet Union.

Sally Kristen Ride was born on May 26, 1951, in Encino, Calif. She showed great early promise as a tennis player, but eventually gave up her plans to play professionally and attended Stanford University. She graduated in 1973 with bachelor's degrees in English and physics. In 1978, as a doctoral candidate and teaching assistant in laser physics at Stanford, she was selected by the National Aeronautics and Space Administration (NASA) as one of six women astronaut candidates. She received a Ph.D. in astrophysics and began her training and evaluation courses that same year. In August 1979 she completed her NASA training, obtained a pilot's license, and became eligible for assignment as a U.S. space shuttle mission specialist.

On June 18, 1983, Ride became the first American woman in space while rocketing into orbit aboard the shuttle orbiter *Challenger*. The shuttle mission lasted six days, during which time she helped deploy two communications satellites and carry out a variety of experiments. She served on a second space mission aboard *Challenger* in October 1984. The crew included another woman, Ride's childhood friend Kathryn Sullivan, who became the first American woman to walk in space.

Ride was training for a third shuttle mission when the *Challenger* exploded after launch in January 1986, a catastrophe that caused NASA to suspend shuttle flights for more than two years. Ride served on the presidential commission appointed to investigate the accident, and she repeated that role as a member of the commission that investigated the in-flight breakup of the orbiter *Columbia* in February 2003.

Ride resigned from NASA in 1987. Two years later she became a professor of physics at the University of California, San

U.S. astronaut and space shuttle specialist Sally Ride, the first American woman to travel into outer space. NASA

Diego, and director of its California Space Institute, serving in that capacity until 1996. In 1999–2000 she held executive positions with Space.com, a Web site presenting space, astronomy, and technology content. Starting in the 1990s, Ride initiated or headed a number of programs and organizations devoted to fostering science in education, particularly to providing support for schoolgirls interested in science, mathematics, or technology. She also wrote or collaborated on several children's books about space exploration and her personal experiences as an astronaut.

CONCLUSION

Humans have always looked at the heavens and wondered about the nature of the objects seen in the night sky. Wonder, as always, prompted a quest for knowledge. Limited to observations by the naked eye, the ancient pioneers in astronomy drew some conclusions that later proved to be false. The most prominent was the Earth-centered model of the universe attributed primarily to Ptolemy, which prevailed for centuries.

Still, the ancient astronomers did work that endured. Hipparchus, for example, made a very accurate calculation of the Moon's distance from Earth. As early as the 3rd century BCE, one astronomer, Aristarchus of Samos, maintained that the Sun is at the center of the universe. This idea was so revolutionary that it still incited controversy even when reintroduced by Copernicus in the 16th century. Galileo's support of the Sun-centered model, based on discoveries made with the newly invented telescope, finally paved the way for the acceptance of this fundamental astronomical fact. The modern age of astronomy had begun.

As a realistic picture of the solar system and the universe evolved, the urge to travel beyond Earth became stronger. In the late 19th and early 20th centuries pioneering rocket scientists such as Konstantin Tsiolkovsky, Hermann Oberth, and Robert H. Goddard began to solve the theoretical and technical problems of space exploration. The historic spaceflight of Soviet cosmonaut Yury Gagarin in 1961 and the U.S. mission to the Moon in 1969 were the culmination of centuries of speculation, study, and hard work. They were also a prelude to several thousands of missions, both manned and unmanned, to investigate the reaches of space beyond Earth's atmosphere.

Although its borders already have been crossed, space still holds mysteries and, undoubtedly, surprises beyond number. The individuals who dedicate themselves to furthering our knowledge of the universe may someday add their names to the list of luminaries profiled in this volume.

GLOSSARY

aerodynamics A branch of dynamics that deals with the motion of air and other gaseous fluids, and with the forces acting on bodies in motion relative to such fluids.

binary Having or based on two parts.

concentric Having a common center.

cosmology A field of study that considers the origin, history, and future of the universe.

dogma A belief or theory held as an established opinion.

ecliptic The great circle that marks the path of the Sun among the stars, or of Earth as seen from the Sun.

equinox Either of the two points on the celestial sphere where the celestial equator intersects the ecliptic.

extragalactic Originating or existing outside the Milky Way galaxy.

heliocentric Having or relating to the Sun as center.

impiety The state of being irreverent or disrespectful, particularly to a supreme being or authority figure.

magnetosphere A region of outer space surrounding a celestial object that is dominated by the object's magnetic field, thus trapping charged particles.

nebula A cloud of gas or dust found in interstellar space.

precession A slow wobble in the orientation of Earth's axis caused by the gravity of the Sun and the Moon.

quintessence Considered the fifth element in ancient times, allegedly the stuff of which all celestial bodies were made.

solstice Either of two points on the ecliptic at which its distance from Earth's equator is greatest.

velocity Quickness of motion; speed.

vocational Of or relating to gaining a skill or trade.

American Astronomical Society (AAS)
2000 Florida Avenue NW, Suite 400
Washington, DC 20009-1231
(202) 328-2010
Web site: http://aas.org
Established 1899, the AAS is the major
   professional organization in North
   America for those interested in
   astronomy. The society shares
   research through its publications,
   conducts professional meetings, and
   helps amateur astronomers polish
   their skills.

Canadian Space Agency (CSA)
John H. Chapman Space Centre
6767 Route de l'Aéroport
Saint-Hubert, QC J3Y 8Y9
Canada
(450) 926-4800
Web site: http://www.asc-csa.gc.ca
The CSA oversees Canada's space program and disseminates information
   about its research to the public through
   its various publications and outreach
   programs.

H.R. MacMillan Space Centre
1100 Chestnut Street
Vancouver, BC V6J 3J9
Canada
(604) 738-7827
Web site: http://www.spacecentre.ca
The H.R. MacMillian Space Centre is
a non-profit community resource in
Vancouver, Canada. It inspires interest
in the universe and space exploration
through innovative programming,
exhibits, and activities.

National Aeronautics and Space
Administration (NASA)
300 E Street SW
Washington, DC 20024
(202) 358-0000
Web site: http://www.nasa.gov
NASA oversees the U.S. space program
and conducts research supporting
innovation in aeronautics and space
exploration.

National Air and Space Museum
Independence Avenue at 6th Street SW
Washington, DC 20560
(202) 633-2214

Web site: http://www.nasm.si.edu
The National Air and Space Museum's extensive collection of historic aircraft and spacecraft recounts the history of aviation and space travel.

U.S. Space and Rocket Center
One Tranquility Base
Huntsville, AL 35805
(800) 63-SPACE (637-7223)
Web site: http://www.rocketcenter.com
The U.S. Space and Rocket Center houses one of the largest collections of rockets and space hardware in the world and chronicles the development of rockets and shuttles. It also runs Space Camp and Aviation Challenge, with programs tailored to students of various ages.

WEB SITES

Due to the changing nature of Internet links, Rosen Educational Services has developed an online list of Web sites related to the subject of this book. This site is updated regularly. Please use this link to access the list:

http://www.rosenlinks.com/inven/astropi

FOR FURTHER READING

Ackroyd, Peter. *Escape from Earth* (Dorling Kindersley, 2004).

Angelo, J.A., Jr. *Human Spaceflight* (Facts on File, 2007).

Carlisle, R.P., and others. *Exploring Space*, rev. ed. (Chelsea House, 2010).

Chaikin, Andrew, and others. *Mission Control, This Is Apollo: The Story of the First Voyages to the Moon* (Viking, 2009).

Furniss, Tim. *A History of Space Exploration* (Mercury, 2005).

Gingerich, Owen, and MacLachlan, J.H. *Nicolaus Copernicus: Making the Earth a Planet* (Oxford Univ. Press, 2005).

Goldsmith, Donald. *The Astronomers* (St. Martin's, 1991).

Gregersen, Erik. *Astronomical Observations: Astronomy and the Study of Deep Space* (Britannica Educational Publishing/ Rosen Education Services, 2010).

Hightower, Paul. *Galileo: Astronomer and Physicist*, rev. ed. (Enslow, 2009).

Jedicke, Peter. *Great Moments in Space Exploration* (Chelsea House, 2007).

Owen, David. *Final Frontier: Voyages into Outer Space* (Firefly, 2004).

Saari, Peggy, and others. *Space Exploration: Biographies* (Thomson Gale, 2005).

INDEX